WORKBOOK:

THE AWE OF GOD

A GUIDE TO USING HEALTHY FEAR OF GOD TO TRANSFORM YOUR LIFE

FOR ALL MY READERS!

TEN STEP GUIDE TO USING HEALTHY FEAR OF GOD TO TRANSFORM YOUR LIFE.

INSTRUCTIONS

1. HAVE A PEN/PENCIL WITH YOU AS YOU STUDY THIS WORKBOOK
2. IN THE "NOTES" SECTION, WRITE DOWN THE THOUGHTS THAT RAN THROUGH YOUR HEAD WHILE NAVIGATING EACH STEP
3. PRACTICE ALL YOU LEARN FROM THIS WORKBOOK.

NAME:

_____

_____

AGE:

_____

JOB:

_____

_____

_____

RELATIONSHIP STATUS:

_____

_____

This is an unendorsed workbook for The Awe of God by John Bevere, which covers every core details of the book.

The human life operates in a sequence and box. Sometimes it goes farther from the box, but the concept of the box still remains.

The only dynamicity we can ever get is a dependent on a supernatural being. He is extraordinary and as such, He gives our lives a deeper meaning and essence.

However, a lot of us do not really know Him. Although, a lot of Christians claim to fear and know Him but the evidence of a deep intimacy is not really seen.

This workbook by Precious Works offers a practical insight on how to build an intimate relationship with God on the foundation of healthy fear in Him.

This book is of great value and a must have for everyone who wants to transform their lives!

STEP 1

"THE FOUNDATION OF FAITH."

The most crucial part of a building is the foundation that was laid. When the foundation is faulty, the building begins to crack because the foundation is the strength of the building.

Christianity basically is like a building and the foundation is on Christ Jesus. If you are going a have a long and strong relationship with Him, it is all dependent of the foundation you have in Him.

What is the foundation of your faith and belief in Him?

What is the foundation of your salvation on Him?

The foundation of your faith remains paramount because it fosters any relationship you can hope to have. That is why you need to ask yourself these questions to deepen your foundation in Him and more importantly, so you'd know the importance and essence of your relationship with Him so you are not pushed neither are you acting on a "whim".

WHAT TO DO?

Take a pen and paper and answer these questions sequentially.

TIPS

When you don't have an answer to these questions, it means your foundation in Him is still shaky and weak.

NOTES

_____

_____

_____

_____

_____

_____

_____

_____

_____

_____

_____

_____

_____

_____

_____

_____

_____

_____

_____

STEP 2

"STUDY."

Like the Word of God said; "Study to show yourself approved, a workman that needs not be ashamed". This only implies that it is only when you know Him that you have confidence in Him and your confidence increases as the knowledge also increases.

Basically, the Word of God is like a treasure trove of infinite knowledge, everything you've needed, you'd ever need and currently need is all in the Word of God. It's just really sad that

you don't have this knowledge
you need to transform your life
daily.

WHAT TO DO?

Make out time daily to study the Word of God.

TIPS

The Word of God is the very substance and essence of life, do not trivialize it.

<u>NOTES</u>

STEP 3

"PRAYER."

Prayers are deeper than the "formal thing" you're used to. To some people, it's all about gathering and talking to God about their problems or even their love for Him.

Well, prayer is basically a "communication." Talking to God about your problems and worries makes all the difference.

He knows you better than anyone else does even better than you know yourself. So He understands you so talk to Him.

WHAT TO DO?

Learn to pray without ceasing.

TIPS

Prayer is basically a heartfelt communication with God and when you pray like that, He'd answer back.

NOTES

_____
_____
_____
_____
_____
_____
_____
_____
_____
_____
_____
_____
_____
_____
_____
_____
_____
_____
_____
_____

STEP 4

"TRUST IN THE LORD."

Trusting in the Lord is not as simply said. It can be really hard when every other element in your life is telling you otherwise.

Like I earlier said, life would be a whole lot easier when we trust in Him because there is simply nothing we can do without Him and we are simply nothing. If He continually supplies the air, we breathe to keep us alive daily what else would He not so for us?

This is more than enough to reverence, trust and fear Him.

WHAT TO DO?

Develop that trust in God even when things are looking bleak.

TIPS

Trust is something that is developed overtime so you have to trust a little more every day.

NOTES

STEP 5

"LOVE."

The Word of God says "For God so loved the world that He gave His Only Begotten Son that whosoever believeth in Him shall have eternal life".
This is truly the height of His Love for us that His Son died so we are not consumed. This is all born out of the Love He has for us.
So why don't we trust Him?
Why is our faith shaky?
The healthy fear of God is born of the love we have for Him, this is the one way to transform your life.

Just as David was a man after God's own heart; it's because David loved with all his being. That is the genuine fear for God.

<u>WHAT TO DO?</u>

Cultivate a good relationship
with God.

<u>TIPS</u>

Intimacy is born out of love.

NOTES

STEP 6

"FREEDOM."

The Word of God sets you free; free from the burdens of this world, the burdens and pains in your life.

This may seem ironic to some people. Because they feel that Christianity is somewhat burdensome and can't set someone free and more importantly, they feel that everything is excessive and controversial.

However, the fear of God can set you free from all other fears in your life. People can be scared of a lot of crazy things but the mere knowledge that those things you're scared of were all created by your Father: Jesus Christ is enough to put you at ease and trust Him.

<u>WHAT TO DO?</u>

Trust in God.

<u>TIPS</u>

Knowledge is power.

<u>NOTES</u>

STEP 7

"UNDERSTANDING."

Understanding is one of the deepest concepts in the world. All the knowledge acquired is useless if there is not the slightest understanding of it.

If you are to acquire anything in life, get understanding. Normally, we'd confess with our mouths that God is the Creator of the Heavens and the Earth but the truth is you don't really understand the depth of that statement.

WHAT TO DO?

Make time out of your day to pray to God daily for broader understanding.

TIPS

Who better to ask for understanding that the Command-Central?

<u>NOTES</u>

_____

_____

_____

_____

_____

_____

_____

_____

_____

_____

_____

_____

_____

_____

_____

_____

_____

_____

_____

STEP 8

"DIVINE DIRECTION."

Whether you believe it or not, healthy fear of God is beneficial. The Word of God says that

"The Fear of God is the beginning of wisdom"... This wisdom being that you have the knowledge that you should fear and reverence Him because of who He is and yet with everything He loves us, with everything He provides for us, with everything He is present for us. His love is enough for us.

The fear of God also fosters divine direction and takes us

away from the confusions in our lives and the confusions of the world in general because He becomes the driver of your lives.

<u>WHAT TO DO?</u>

Let God in fully.

<u>TIPS</u>

Don't seclude Him to just one
part of your life.

<u>NOTES</u>

_____

_____

_____

_____

_____

_____

_____

_____

_____

_____

_____

_____

_____

_____

_____

_____

_____

_____

STEP 9

"BE GRATEFUL."

A heart full of gratitude will always receive more. Even if the situation seems hopeless right now, just think back to all the instances He has saved you in the past. The fear of God is all dependent on how best you know.

When you understand how big He is, how pure He is and yet He forgives us. The Creator of the Heavens and Earth has assured us that He'd be with us till the end of the age; He loves us and

for this we'd be eternally
grateful.

<u>WHAT TO DO?</u>

Learn to be grateful even in the little things He has done for you.

<u>TIPS</u>

You'd be more grateful when you know more about Him.

NOTES

STEP 10

"BUILD A COMMUNITY"

Everyone needs a companion every now and then. No man is an island. That only goes to say that we are social beings and we can't function effectively in our lives by ourselves alone.

In the same vain, it is important to have people around that "speak your language"; not literally though.

When you're looking to transform your life and every angle of it all dependent on your belief and faith in God, you need people like minded people around you. These people understand the struggles that come with it as well as the joys. You can form a little youth community in your church; where you help each other grow in faith.

<u>WHAT TO DO?</u>

Get like-minded people so you can easily flow.

<u>TIPS</u>

Be humble to learn from other people.

NOTES

THE END OF THIS WORKBOOK.

AFTER FOLLOWING THE ABOVE-STATED STEPS, EVALUATE YOURSELF AND REPEAT THE SAME STEPS!

HOW HAS THIS WORKBOOK HELPED YOU?

_____

_____

_____

_____

_____

_____

_____

_____

_____

_____

_____

_____

_____

_____

_____

_____

<u>PRIVATE NOTES</u>

EXTRAS

Made in United States
Troutdale, OR
01/04/2024

16702566R00029